THE WHISTLE STOP PARTY

For Dear Peg
Driver, Guard and Stoker

COLLINS PUBLISHERS AUSTRALIA
First published by William Collins Pty. Ltd., Sydney
in association with Anne Ingram Books.

© Text Nan Hunt 1990
© Illustrations Craig Smith 1990

Typeset by Focusgraphics
in Baskerville 15 point

National Library of Australia
Cataloguing in Publication Data

Hunt, Nan.
The whistle stop party.
For children
ISBN 0 7322 4944 9
I. Smith, Craig, II. Title.
A823'.3

THE WHISTLE STOP PARTY

by Nan Hunt

Illustrations by Craig Smith

COLLINS PUBLISHERS AUSTRALIA
in association with
ANNE INGRAM BOOKS

In all her life Mrs Millie Mack could not remember such a cold summer. Here it was December and she was still in her woollies. One cold night she had to have a fire. When the kindling caught alight and began to *crickle crackle,* Tom Bola purred.

There were two pieces of the half door from a bogey louvre in the wood box, and Mrs Millie Mack put one on the flames. Almost immediately there was an urgent whistle up the chimney. It went on whistling all the way down as the Express came slowly out into the room hissing and blowing steam, and . . .

STOPPED!

Mrs Millie Mack could hardly believe her eyes.

The driver raised his hat. 'Dear Mrs Millie Mack,' he said, 'you know Mick, the guard on the Mixed Goods? He's retiring and the local loco people want to give him a party . . .'

'Here? Oh do have it here!'

'You're sure? That's great. I'll tell the others. It's to be a surprise for Mick. How about tomorrow night?'

'Couldn't be better,' Mrs Millie Mack said.

'See you then. Coming for a ride, Tom?' The cat pretended he hadn't heard and the driver laughed and set the train in motion.

With a great grunting of

HAM'n eggs HARIcots HORSEradish HONey

the Express went off down the hall, through the door and away into the night.

Next morning Mrs Millie Mack was up at daybreak picking flowers, dusting and vacuuming and tidying. While she ate breakfast she made a list.

Then she began to cook.

She made boiled fruit cake, date ring with lemon sugar topping, orange cake, apple tea cake, fairy cakes, biscuits, jelly sponge, cream puffs, lamingtons, lemon cheese tarts, and Chester cake dripping juice. At the very end a batch of meringues went into the oven to use up the last of the heat.

Mrs Millie Mack was exhausted. She had to have a cup of tea and a Vegemite and alfalfa sprout sandwich to revive her.

Mrs Millie Mack set the table with the best lace cloth. On a side cupboard she put out all the glasses. She wrapped up some handkerchiefs she had really bought to give the Postman for Christmas and wrote a card for Mick.

As soon as it was dark she lit the fire, throwing on the very last piece of the half door from a bogey louvre, and went to the kitchen to check the sausage rolls and party pies and asparagus puffs already heating in the oven. The sandwiches were ready, and on the stove a boiler full of frankfurts simmered in a red glow.

The Express came first, whooshing out of the chimney, through the room, down the hall and out into the street, where it stopped. The train crew came inside after wiping their feet carefully on the mat. The guard carried a lantern with green glass on one side and red on the other.

They heard the Mixed Goods coming and the guard from the Express picked up his signalling lantern and hurried outside.

ar car-ACK ar car-ICK ar car-ACK ar car-ICK

clanked the train, the driver giving Mrs Millie Mack a big wink as it went slowly down the hall. The brakes squeaked as it stopped, and Mick was arguing about timetables and saying he couldn't possibly run late on his very last day.

Soon afterwards the four-coach all-stations passenger train gave its funny snort-scream whistle, and trundled out into the room, stopping with its front outside the garden gate and its back inside the hall. Out tumbled the passengers carrying balloons and blowing party whistles and shouting, 'Where's Mick?'

'He's here!' the Express driver said, giving Mick a push.

'Surprise! Surprise!' everyone shouted.

Mick's mouth fell open with astonishment. He looked at the people, he looked at the party food, he looked at the big notice,

HAPPY RETIREMENT MICK

and wiped a speck of soot out of his eyes.

'Is everybody here?'

'We're waiting for the push-up.'

'Aren't we always?' muttered the driver of the Mixed Goods, rolling his eyes.

'And here she comes!'

A packet   a picket   a packet of barley
Girhacket   girhicket
Arr umble   arr imble
Arr   WHEE-whee-*weep*.

Out panted the engine, the driver grinning all over his face.

'Park it up the hall,' ordered the Express guard, 'and hurry up.'

'Do help yourselves,' Mrs Millie Mack said. 'There's plenty more in the kitchen.'

The company needed no further invitation and soon everyone was eating and talking.

'Hi cat!' Mick said, as Tom purred round his legs. 'Been off on any more train rides, hmm? You'd best come with me next time, it's safer in the Guard's Van.' He choked on a sandwich, remembering he was on his last run.

Before Mick could get too sad, one of the drivers spoke up. 'Safer, Mick? What about that time the pup got loose?'

Mick laughed. 'I'd forgotten that. He chewed his way out of the pet carry carton he was in and ate the side out of a box full of half-grown cockerels.'

'He didn't!'

'He did so! The air was full of squawks and feathers and swears and barks. In the end I had both hands full of upside down chooks with the pup clawing up me pants leg trying to get at 'em.'

'I'm going to be a guard when I grow up,' said a girl. 'I think it would be fun.'

'Not all fun,' said the fireman of the Express. 'Getting out of bed all hours of the night to do your shift. Sleeping in daylight. Never there to see your kids.'

'Trains do things, too,' said a driver. 'I remember once a loco dropped its steam going up Raglan Hill. A crew never lives down something like that.'

'And they'll jump off the track just to nark you, if there's so much as a piece of metal on the line,' said another. 'Remember the wheat train that took to the scrub near Sodwalls? Wheat everywhere, and every parrot west of the Dividing Range came to the party! The gangers had to lay a new section round *that* mess.'

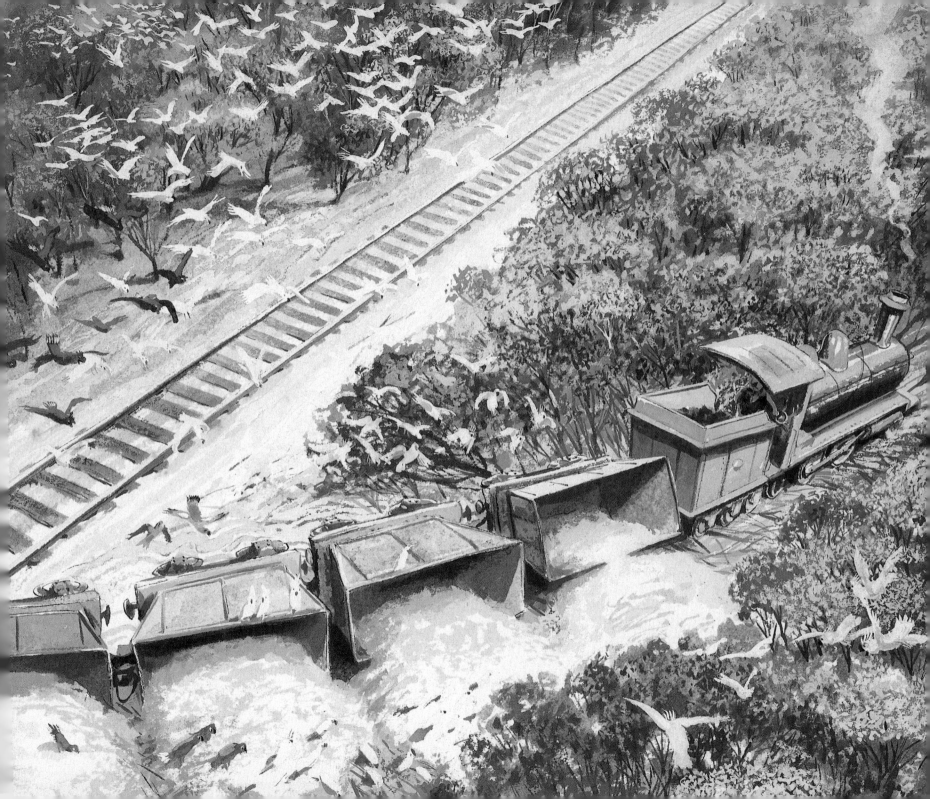

'What's the funniest thing ever happened to you, Mick?'

'I've been on the railway, man and boy, for fifty years,' Mick said, rubbing his chin. 'You forget a lot. But I'll never forget one time during the war when we lost a troop train. We'd been taking troops north non-stop. Working double shifts, some of us, everyone tired. The soldiers were noisy, but settled down after dark and we just rattled along, rattled along, rattled along, biddly dum . . .'

'Hey, Mick! Wake up!'

'Sorry. Just remembering makes me tired! I know I went to sleep that night. When the sun came up I looked out and we're bang smack in the middle of nowhere, and the driver comes walking up alongside the train.

'"Mick," says he, "do you know where we are?" "You're driving," I said. "There's a sandhill across the line and nothing the other side of it. Not a rail, not a sleeper, not anything. We'll have to back up." So we backed that train and backed that train and backed that train to the junction where someone had thrown the wrong lever and put us on an abandoned mine line. And all the way, the troops were singing out for their breakfusses, an' I mean singing out! The army was searching for us. The railway heads were screaming. I mean to say, you can't just lose a train into thin air, they said. Can't be done, they said. But it can, because we did it!'

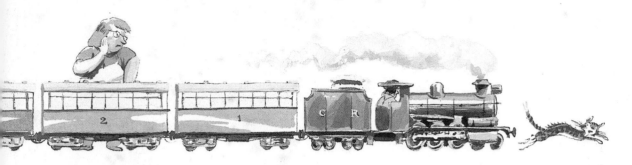

The Express driver checked his watch, cleared his throat, and asked Mick to stand out in front, please. He made a long speech about Guards, especially Mick, and about not having to go to work any more, and would Mick kindly accept a gold watch and chain with best wishes from all his mates.

Everyone cheered and clapped and sang *For he's a jolly good fellow* and crowded round to shake Mick's hand.

Mick stood there, suddenly tongue-tied, until his driver gave him a poke and said, 'Speak up, Mick'.

All in a rush Mick said, 'It's been the best night of me whole life, fair dinkum, and I don't know how to thank you. You're a beaut lot of mates, the best a man could have. We've shared tough times and good times and funny times, but we've shared them. It's been a beaut party, Mrs Millie, with beaut food, and everything's beaut. I dunno what else to say . . . so thank you.'

'Time to go, lads,' the Express driver said. 'A vote of thanks to you, Mrs Millie Mack, from all present. See you next time. . .'

The Express took off with a *chutch-chutch-chutch* as the steam powered the pistons on the driving wheels. The Mixed Goods followed, Mick looking anxiously at the time on his new gold watch. The passengers scrambled back into the all-stations passenger train, and in no time it slid away down the hall, through the door and away into the night. The pink push-up engine was low in steam and grumbled,

Git orf of me ankles me ankles me ankles

judder judder judder

Git ORF of me ankles

as it clanked off after the others.

Mrs Millie Mack made herself a fresh pot of tea, kicked off her shoes, and sat beside the fireplace, tired but happy. Tom jumped up on her lap. After a while Mrs Millie Mack put down her cup, and . . . was it only a dream, or did she really hear the train song echoing up the chimney?

Clicketty clack   clicketty clack
Clicketty clicketty clicketty clack
Steaming along on the per way track
All the way from the city and back
Over the points
     gerunk gerunk gerunk
Pickemup pickemup hurry along
Biddly dum de biddly dong
This is the roundabout railerway song . . .